# PABLO NERUDA
## *Fully Empowered*

TRANSLATED, WITH A NEW INTRODUCTION, BY
## ALASTAIR REID

A NEW DIRECTIONS BOOK

Alastair Reid's translations of certain of these poems previ-
ously appeared in *Pablo Neruda: Selected Poems,* published
originally by Delacorte Press/Seymour Lawrence; in *Pablo
Neruda: A New Decade,* published by Grossman Publishers.
Grateful acknowledgment is made to these publishers for
permission to reprint.

This volume is published by arrangement with
Farrar, Straus & Giroux, Inc.

First published paperbound as New Directions Paperbook
792 in 1995.

Manufactured in the United States of America.
Published simultaneously in Canada by
Penguin Books Canada Limited.
New Directions Books are printed on acid-free paper.

Library of Congress Cataloging-in-Publication Data
        Neruda, Pablo, 1904-1973.
[Plenos poderes. English] Fully empowered/Pablo Neruda ;
translated by Alastair Reid.
        p. cm.        — (New Directions paperbook ; 792)
"A New Directions book."   English and Spanish.
        ISBN 0-8112-1281-5 (alk. paper)
I. Reid, Alastair, 1926-    . II. Title.
PQ8097.N4P5513   1995     94-7998
861—dc20                CIP

New Directions Books are published for James Laughlin
by New Directions Publishing Corporation,
80 Eighth Avenue, New York 10011

THIRD PRINTING

# CONTENTS

Pablo Neruda lived many lives as a poet, shedding each one, and its accompanying poetic manner, as a lizard sheds a skin, and emerging always with new insights, new attitudes, and new poems. *Plenos Poderes* (*Fully Empowered*) came at the height of a period in Neruda's life which Neruda himself would refer to as his "autumn," an autumn, however, that was both mellow and fruitful. He had come to rest in Chile in the mid-fifties in his house in Isla Negra, which stood on a low bluff above the beach looking out to the Pacific. The house, where he lived with Matilde Urrutia, his third wife, was furnished with the objects Neruda had collected or brought back from his travels—ships' figureheads, ships in bottles, shells, clocks, postcards, a giant shoe that had once hung outside a cobbler's in Temuco, a full size papier-mâché horse, nautical instruments: these objects formed the vocabulary of many of his poems. He flew his own flag from a yardarm in his garden whenever he was in residence. Friends would come frequently to visit, and he would preside over succulent lunches that he himself had cooked, reciting poems to the company, disappearing at intervals into his writing room, where poems never stopped flowing from him. For him, it was a rich and fulfilling time.

The poems he wrote at that time turned over a remarkable new leaf. For each of the vast poetic enterprises Neruda had previously taken on, like his *Canto General* or his three books of Odes, he had developed an appropriate manner. They were in a sense "public" works, vast collections of poems with a common theme. Now, he turned to writing a wholly personal poetry, single lyrics, often short, sometimes whimsical and self-mocking, adventurous in form, and exceedingly miscellaneous in subject matter. The first collection of these newly personal poems, *Estravagario,* appeared in 1958, and both startled and delighted his readers. *Estravagario* remained for Neruda a favorite among his books. No longer was he undertaking the dutiful political poems of an earlier decade, although politics intrude frequently into the personal. The poems are often self-questioning, self-defining: in them, Neruda sets his awareness in a wholly personal context, and in the physical landscape of Isla Negra, with which the poems are saturated. They are in the main warm and affecting poems, and in them, Neruda rehumanizes himself as "a man rainy and happy, lively and autumn-minded."

*Fully Empowered* was the second book of personal poems to come out of that period. Published in September of 1962, it has the same miscellaneous nature as *Estravagario,* the same wide range of themes and forms. Some earlier manners reappear, as in the exquisite miniature "Ode to Ironing," and the wonderfully extravagant Ode to his friend, the eccentric composer Acario Cotapos. Embedded in the book is also one public poem, "El Pueblo," written by Neruda for the Congress of the Chilean Communist Party, which is a quite magnificent restatement of dogma in the form of high poetry and must stand as one of his most "important" poems. There are, however, two lyrics in *Fully Empowered* in which Neruda makes serious and moving personal statements. In "The Poet's Obligation," he restates what has been his declared purpose since *The Heights of Macchu Picchu*: to be in his poems a voice for all those people—and things—that have no voice: that is the poet's obligation. In "Fully Empowered," he fortifies this declaration of faith in poetry, although the light in his poems is now tempered by a growing awareness of shadow, of the dark as an inevitable accompaniment to light. There is also a handful of beautifully fashioned short lyrics that invoke aspects of Isla Negra—times of day, miniature landscapes, atmospheres—and a number of poems that summon up the sprawling port of Valparaíso, up the coast from Isla Negra, which Neruda rediscovered in those years. One of the poems is addressed to La Sebastiana, the eccentric house Neruda built on top of a cinema, with an all-embracing view of the port. There are also some of his most beautiful single lyrics, like "The Past," "Goodbyes," and "To Sorrow," that come from a wiser and more reflective Neruda, and have a new and confident grace to them, as if, as one Latin American critic remarked, "the poet were repossessing himself."

As with all the work of Neruda, the main challenge for the translator is to capture that tone of his that makes his poetry always so distinctive. While I was translating his work, I spent many hours listening intently to his voice, in conversation, on tape, till I could hear it at will. His poems are always spoken poems, and it is for the translator to supply, in whatever language he is working into, a proper equivalent for that mesmerizing original.

Two instances need comment, however. The first is the title of the poem "El Pueblo." The word "pueblo" invokes in Spanish much more than either a place or the people who inhabit it: it humanizes a place as a state of being, as a set of values and allegiances. It deserves to be left alone, untranslated: English has nothing quite as embracing. The other concerns the book's title. "Plenos poderes" are the powers delegated to an ambassador to empower him in his office, as in the English word "plenipotentiary." Since Neruda had been a diplomat from his early twenties, he wore the phrase well; but he was also referring to his poetic powers, which he felt were then at their height. English had to supply a phrase that contained both senses, and that still carried the formality that "plenos poderes" does in Spanish. I pondered for a very long time before stumbling on "fully empowered" as a satisfactory solution.

*Fully Empowered* is a very satisfying nutshell volume, so shifting is its focus, so varied its style, from the grand manner to the most intimate. Translating it was an immersion that gave me intense pleasure.

Alastair Reid

*Fully Empowered*

# Deber del poeta

A quien no escucha el mar en este viernes
por la mañana, a quien adentro de algo,
casa, oficina, fábrica o mujer,
o calle o mina o seco calabozo:
a éste yo acudo y sin hablar ni ver
llego y abro la puerta del encierro
y un sin fin se oye vago en la insistencia,
un largo trueno roto se encadena
al peso del planeta y de la espuma,
surgen los ríos roncos del océano,
vibra veloz en su rosal la estrella
y el mar palpita, muere y continúa.

Así por el destino conducido
debo sin tregua oír y conservar
el lamento marino en mi conciencia,
debo sentir el golpe de agua dura
y recogerlo en una taza eterna
para que donde esté el encarcelado,
donde sufra el castigo del otoño
yo esté presente con una ola errante,
yo circule a través de las ventanas
y al oírme levante la mirada
diciendo: cómo me acercaré al océano?
Y yo transmitiré sin decir nada
los ecos estrellados de la ola,
un quebranto de espuma y arenales,
un susurro de sal que se retira,
el grito gris del ave de la costa.

Y así, por mí, la libertad y el mar
responderán al corazón oscuro.

# The Poet's Obligation

To whoever is not listening to the sea
this Friday morning, to whoever is cooped up
in house or office, factory or woman
or street or mine or dry prison cell,
to him I come, and without speaking or looking
I arrive and open the door of his prison,
and a vibration starts up, vague and insistent,
a long rumble of thunder adds itself
to the weight of the planet and the foam,
the groaning rivers of the ocean rise,
the star vibrates quickly in its corona
and the sea beats, dies, and goes on beating.

So, drawn on by my destiny,
I ceaselessly must listen to and keep
the sea's lamenting in my consciousness,
I must feel the crash of the hard water
and gather it up in a perpetual cup
so that, wherever those in prison may be,
wherever they suffer the sentence of the autumn,
I may be present with an errant wave,
I may move in and out of windows,
and hearing me, eyes may lift themselves,
asking "How can I reach the sea?"
And I will pass to them, saying nothing,
the starry echoes of the wave,
a breaking up of foam and quicksand,
a rustling of salt withdrawing itself,
the gray cry of sea birds on the coast.

So, through me, freedom and the sea
will call in answer to the shrouded heart.

# La palabra

Nació
la palabra en la sangre,
creció en el cuerpo oscuro, palpitando,
y voló con los labios y la boca.

Más lejos y más cerca
aún, aún venía
de padres muertos y de errantes razas,
de territorios que se hicieron piedra,
que se cansaron de sus pobres tribus,
porque cuando el dolor salió al camino
los pueblos anduvieron y llegaron
y nueva tierra y agua reunieron
para sembrar de nuevo su palabra.
Y así la herencia es ésta:
éste es el aire que nos comunica
con el hombre enterrado y con la aurora
de nuevos seres que aún no amanecieron.

Aún la atmósfera tiembla
con la primera palabra
elaborada
con pánico y gemido.
Salió
de las tinieblas
y hasta ahora no hay trueno
que truene aún con su ferretería
como aquella palabra,
la primera
palabra pronunciada:
tal vez sólo un susurro fue, una gota,

# The Word

The word
was born in the blood,
grew in the dark body, beating,
and took flight through the lips and the mouth.

Farther away and nearer
still, still it came
from dead fathers and from wandering races,
from lands which had turned to stone,
lands weary of their poor tribes,
for when grief took to the roads
the people set out and arrived
and married new land and water
to grow their words again.
And so this is the inheritance;
this is the wavelength which connects us
with dead men and the dawning
of new beings not yet come to light.

Still the atmosphere quivers
with the first word uttered
dressed up
in terror and sighing.
It emerged
from the darkness
and until now there is no thunder
that ever rumbles with the iron voice
of that word,
the first
word uttered—
perhaps it was only a ripple, a single drop,

y cae y cae aún su catarata.

Luego el sentido llena la palabra.
Quedó preñada y se llenó de vidas,
Todo fue nacimientos y sonidos :
la afirmación, la claridad, la fuerza,
la negación, la destrucción, la muerte :
el verbo asumió todos los poderes
y se fundió existencia con esencia
en la electricidad de su hermosura.

Palabra humana, sílaba, cadera
de larga luz y dura platería,
hereditaria copa que recibe
las comunicaciones de la sangre :
he aquí que el silencio fue integrado
por el total de la palabra humana
y no hablar es morir entre los seres :
se hace lenguaje hasta la cabellera,
habla la boca sin mover los labios :
los ojos de repente son palabras.

Yo tomo la palabra y la recorro
como si fuera sólo forma humana,
me embelesan sus líneas y navego
en cada resonancia del idioma :
pronuncio y soy y sin hablar me acerca
el fin de las palabras al silencio.

Bebo por la palabra levantando
una palabra o copa cristalina,
en ella bebo

and yet its great cataract falls and falls.

Later on, the word fills with meaning.
Always with child, it filled up with lives.
Everything was births and sounds—
affirmation, clarity, strength,
negation, destruction, death—
the verb took over all the power
and blended existence with essence
in the electricity of its grace.

Human word, syllable, flank
of extending light and solid silverwork,
hereditary goblet which receives
the communications of the blood—
here is where silence came together with
the wholeness of the human word,
and, for human beings, not to speak is to die—
language extends even to the hair,
the mouth speaks without the lips moving,
all of a sudden, the eyes are words.

I take the word and pass it through my senses
as though it were no more than a human shape;
its arrangements awe me and I find my way
through each resonance of the spoken word—
I utter and I am and, speechless, I approach
across the edge of words silence itself.

I drink to the word, raising
a word or a shining cup;
in it I drink

el vino del idioma
o el agua interminable,
manantial maternal de las palabras,
y copa y agua y vino
originan mi canto
porque el verbo es origen
y vierte vida : es sangre,
es la sangre que expresa su substancia
y está dispuesto así su desarrollo :
dan cristal al cristal, sangre a la sangre,
y dan vida a la vida las palabras.

the pure wine of language
or inexhaustible water,
maternal source of words,
and cup and water and wine
give rise to my song
because the verb is the source
and vivid life—it is blood,
blood which expresses its substance
and so ordains its own unwinding.
Words give glass quality to glass, blood to blood,
and life to life itself.

# Océano

Cuerpo más puro que un ola,
sal que lava la línea,
y el ave lúcida
volando sin raíces.

# Ocean

Body more perfect than a wave,
salt washing the sea line,
and the shining bird
flying without ground roots.

# Agua

Todo en la tierra se encrespó, la zarza
clavó y el hilo verde
mordía, el pétalo cayó cayendo
hasta que única flor fue la caída.
El agua es diferente,
no tiene dirección sino hermosura,
corre por cada sueño de color,
toma lecciones claras
de la piedra
y en esos menesteres elabora
los deberes intactos de la espuma.

# Water

Everything on the earth bristled, the bramble
pricked and the green thread
nibbled away, the petal fell, falling
until the only flower was the falling itself.
Water is another matter,
has no direction but its own bright grace,
runs through all imaginable colors,
takes limpid lessons
from stone,
and in those functionings plays out
the unrealized ambitions of the foam.

# El mar

Un solo ser, pero no hay sangre.
Una sola caricia, muerte o rosa.
Viene el mar y reúne nuestras vidas
y solo ataca y se reparte y canta
en noche y día y hombre y criatura.
La esencia : fuego y frío : movimiento.

# The Sea

A single entity, but no blood.
A single caress, death or a rose.
The sea comes in and puts our lives together
and attacks alone and spreads itself and sings
in nights and days and men and living creatures.
Its essence—fire and cold; movement, movement.

## Nace

Yo aquí vine a los límites
en donde no hay que decir nada,
todo se aprende con tiempo y océano,
y volvía la luna,
sus líneas plateadas
y cada vez se rompía la sombra
con un golpe de ola
y cada día en el balcón del mar
abre las alas, nace el fuego
y todo sigue azul como mañana.

# It Is Born

Here I came to the very edge
where nothing at all needs saying,
everything is absorbed through weather and the sea,
and the moon swam back,
its rays all silvered,
and time and again the darkness would be broken
by the crash of a wave,
and every day on the balcony of the sea,
wings open, fire is born,
and everything is blue again like morning.

## Torre

La línea lava el mundo,
oh inmutable frescura,
oh larga espada :
cortas
el desorden,
allí queda el naufragio,
aquí la estrella,
de punto a punto a punto
circula por la línea
la pureza
y es invariable el clima,
segura la medida,
firme el muro del ángulo
mientras el aire cambia y cruza
la torre
pura
de la geometría.

# Tower

The sea line washes the world.
Oh, immutable newness,
oh, great sword—
you cut clean through
disorder;
there the shipwreck is left,
there the star.
From point to point to point
cleanness
runs along the sea line,
and it is unvarying, its climate,
it is reliable, its exactness,
it is solid, its curved division,
while the air is changing and crossing
the clear
tower
of its geometry.

## Planeta

Hay piedras de agua en la luna?
Hay aguas de oro?
De qué color es el otoño?
Se unen uno a uno los días
hasta que en una cabellera
se desenlazan? Cuánto cae
—papeles, vino, manos, muertos—
de la tierra en esa comarca?

Viven allí los ahogados?

# Planet

Are there stones of water on the moon?
Are there waters of gold?
What color is autumn?
Do the days run into one another
until like a shock of hair
they all unravel? How much falls
—paper, wine, hands, dead bodies—
from the earth on that far place?

Is it there that the drowned live?

## El desnudo

Esta raya es el Sur que corre,
este círculo es el Oeste,
las madejas las hizo el viento
con sus capítulos más claros
y es recto el mediodía como
un mástil que sostiene el cielo
mientras vuelan las líneas puras
de silencio en silencio hasta ser
las aves delgadas del aire,
las direcciones de la dicha.

# Naked

This ray is the running sun,
this circle is the East—
tangles the wind made
on its most limpid errands,
and noon is high and upright,
a mast supporting the sky,
while the clear arrows fly
from silence to silence till they are
the slim birds of the air,
the lines that luck takes.

## En la torre

En esta grave torre
no hay combate:
la niebla, el aire, el día
la rodearon, se fueron
y me quedé con cielo y con papel,
solitarias dulzuras y deberes.
Pura torre de tierra
con odio y mar lejanos
removida
por la ola del cielo:
en la línea, en la palabra cuántas
sílabas? He dicho?

Bella es la incertidumbre del rocío,
en la mañana cae
separando
la noche de la aurora
y su glacial regalo
permanece
indeciso, esperando el duro sol
que lo herirá de muerte.
No se sabe
si cerramos los ojos o la noche
abre en nosotros ojos estrellados,
si cava en la pared de nuestro sueño
hasta que abre una puerta.
Pero el sueño
es el veloz vestido de un minuto:
se gastó en un latido
de la sombra
y cayó a nuestros pies, deshabitado,

## In the Tower

In this most solemn tower
there is no struggle.
The fog, the air, the day
surrounded it and left
and I stayed with sky and paper,
solitary joys and debts.
Clear tower of earth
with hate and the sea at a distance
stirred
by waves in the sky.
How many syllables in the line,
in the word? Did I say?

Beautiful the accident of the dew—
it falls at morning
separating
the night from the dawn
and its icy offering
hangs on
uncertainly, waiting for sharp sun
to do it to death.
It's hard to tell
if we close our eyes or if night
opens in us other starred eyes,
if it burrows into the wall of our dream
till some door opens.
But the dream
is only the flitting costume of one moment,
is spent in one beat
of the darkness,
and falls at our feet, cast off

cuando se mueve el día y nos navega.

Ésta es la torre desde donde veo
entre la luz y el agua sigilosa
al tiempo con su espada
y me apresuro entonces a vivir,
respiro todo el aire,
me enajena el desierto
que se construye sobre la ciudad
y hablo conmigo sin saber con quién
deshojando el silencio
de la altura.

as the day stirs and sails away with us.

This is the tower from which I watch,
between the light and the tight-lipped water,
time with its sword,
and then I rush to live,
I breathe all the air,
I am stunned by the desert
building up over the city
and I speak to myself without knowing who I am,
stripping the leaves from the silence
of the high places.

# Pájaro

Caía de un pájaro a otro
todo lo que el día trae,
iba de flauta en flauta el día,
iba vestido de verdura
con vuelos que abrían un túnel,
y por allí pasaba el viento
por donde las aves abrían
el aire compacto y azul :
por allí entraba la noche.

Cuando volví de tantos viajes
me quedé suspendido y verde
entre el sol y la geografía :
vi cómo trabajan las alas,
cómo se transmite el perfume
por un telégrafo emplumado
y desde arriba vi el camino,
los manantiales, las tejas,
los pescadores a pescar,
los pantalones de la espuma,
todo desde mi cielo verde.
No tenía más alfabeto
que el viaje de las golondrinas,
el agua pura y pequeñita
del pequeño pájaro ardiendo
que baila saliendo del polen.

# Bird

It was passed from one bird to another,
the whole gift of the day.
The day went from flute to flute,
went dressed in vegetation,
in flights which opened a tunnel
through which the wind would pass
to where birds were breaking open
the dense blue air—
and there, night came in.

When I returned from so many journeys,
I stayed suspended and green
between sun and geography—
I saw how wings worked,
how perfumes are transmitted
by feathery telegraph,
and from above I saw the path,
the springs and the roof tiles,
the fishermen at their trades,
the trousers of the foam ;
I saw it all from my green sky.
I had no more alphabet
than the swallows in their courses,
the tiny, shining water
of the small bird on fire
which dances out of the pollen.

## Serenata

Con la mano recojo este vacío,
imponderable noche, familias estrelladas,
un coro más callado que el silencio,
un sonido de luna, algo secreto, un triángulo,
un trapecio de tiza.
Es la noche oceánica, la soledad tercera,
una vacilación abriendo puertas, alas,
la población profunda que no tiene presencia
palpita desbordando los nombres del estuario.

Noche, nombre del mar, patria, racimo, rosa!

# Serenade

With my hand I gather in this emptiness,
the bewildering night, the starry families,
a chorus still more silent than the silence,
a moon sound, something secret, a triangle,
a chalked geometry.
It is the night of the ocean, the third solitude,
a quivering which opens doors and wings.
The mysterious and intangible population
trembles and washes over the names of the estuary.

Night, the sea's name, homeland, roots, rose!

# El constructor

Yo escogí la quimera,
de sal helada construí la estatua :
fundé el reloj en plena lluvia
y vivo sin embargo.

Es verdad que mi largo poderío
subdividió los sueños
y sin que yo supiera levantaban
muros, separaciones, incesantes.

Entonces fui a la costa.

Yo vi cuando nació la embarcación,
la toqué, lisa como el pez sagrado :
tembló como la cítara de Dios,
la madera era pura,
tenía olor a miel.
Y cuando no volvía,
la nave no volvía,
todos se sumergieron en sus lágrimas
mientras yo regresaba a la madera
con el hacha desnuda como estrella.

Mi religión eran aquellas naves

No tengo más remedio que vivir.

# The Builder

I chose my own illusion,
from frozen salt I made its likeness—
I based my time on the great rain
and, even so, I am still alive.

It is true that my long mastery
divided up the dreams
and without my knowing there arose
walls, separations, endlessly.

Then I went to the coast.

I saw the beginnings of the ship,
I touched it, smooth as the sacred fish—
it quivered like the harp of heaven,
the woodwork was clean,
it had the scent of honey.
And when it did not come back,
the ship did not come back,
everyone drowned in his own tears
while I went back to the wood
with an ax naked as a star.

My faith lay in those ships.

I have no recourse but to live.

# Para lavar a un niño

Sólo el amor más viejo de la tierra
lava y peina la estatua de los niños,
endereza las piernas, las rodillas,
sube el agua, resbalan los jabones,
y el cuerpo puro sale a respirar
el aire de la flor y de la madre.

Oh vigilancia clara !
Oh dulce alevosía !
Oh tierna guerra !

Ya el pelo era un tortuoso
pelaje entrecruzado por carbones,
por aserrín y aceite,
por hollines, alambres y cangrejos,
hasta que la paciencia
del amor
estableció los cubos, las esponjas,
los peines, las toallas,
y de fregar y de peinar y de ámbar,
de antigua parsimonia y de jazmines
quedó más nuevo el niño todavía
y corrió de las manos de la madre
a montarse de nuevo en su ciclón,
a buscar lodo, aceite, orines, tinta,
a herirse y revolcarse entre las piedras.
Y así recién lavado salta el niño a vivir
porque más tarde sólo tendrá tiempo
para andar limpio, pero ya sin vida.

# To Wash a Child

Love, the most immemorial on earth,
washes and combs the effigy of the children,
straightens the feet and knees;
the water rises, the soap slithers,
and the pristine body emerges to breathe
the air of flowers and the mother.

Oh, the sharp watchfulness,
the sweet deceptions,
the loving struggle!

Now the hair is a tangled
pelt crisscrossed by charcoal,
by sawdust and oil,
soot, wires, and crabs,
until love patiently,
patiently,
sets up buckets and sponges,
combs and towels,
and from scrubbing and combing and amber,
from ancient scruples and from jasmine,
emerges the child, cleaner than ever,
running from the mother's arms
to clamber again on its whirlwind,
to look for mud, oil, piss, and ink,
to hurt itself, tumble about on the stones.
In that way, newly washed, the child leaps into life;
for later it will have time for nothing more
than keeping clean, but lifelessly by then.

## Oda para planchar

La poesía es blanca :
sale del agua envuelta en gotas,
se arruga y se amontona,
hay que extender la piel de este planeta,
hay que planchar el mar de su blancura
y van y van las manos,
se alisan las sagradas superficies
y así se hacen las cosas :
las manos hacen cada día el mundo,
se une el fuego al acero,
llegan el lino, el lienzo y el tocuyo
del combate de las lavanderías
y nace de la luz una paloma :
la castidad regresa de la espuma.

# In Praise of Ironing

Poetry is pure white.
It emerges from water covered with drops,
is wrinkled, all in a heap.
It has to be spread out, the skin of this planet,
has to be ironed out, the sea's whiteness;
and the hands keep moving, moving,
the holy surfaces are smoothed out,
and that is how things are accomplished.
Every day, hands are creating the world,
fire is married to steel,
and canvas, linen, and cotton come back
from the skirmishings of the laundries,
and out of light a dove is born—
pure innocence returns out of the swirl.

# Los nacimientos

Nunca recordaremos haber muerto.

Tanta paciencia
para ser tuvimos
anotando
los números, los días,
los años y los meses,
los cabellos, las bocas que besamos,
y aquel minuto de morir
lo dejaremos sin anotación :
se lo damos a otros de recuerdo
o simplemente al agua,
al agua, al aire, al tiempo.
Ni de nacer tampoco
guardamos la memoria,
aunque importante y fresco fue ir naciendo :
y ahora no recuerdas un detalle,
no has guardado ni un ramo
de la primera luz.

Se sabe que nacemos.

Se sabe que en la sala
o en el bosque
o en el tugurio del barrio pesquero
o en los cañaverales crepitantes
hay un silencio enteramente extraño,
un minuto solemne de madera

# Births

We will never have any memory of dying.

We were so patient
about our being,
noting down
numbers, days,
years and months,
hair, and the mouths we kiss,
and that moment of dying
we let pass without a note—
we leave it to others as memory,
or we leave it simply to water,
to water, to air, to time.
Nor do we even keep
the memory of being born,
although to come into being was tumultuous and new ;
and now you don't remember a single detail
and haven't kept even a trace
of your first light.

It's well known that we are born.

It's well known that in the room
or in the wood
or in the shelter in the fishermen's quarter
or in the rustling canefields
there is a quite unusual silence,
a grave and wooden moment as

y una mujer se dispone a parir.

Se sabe que nacimos.

Pero de la profunda sacudida
de no ser a existir, a tener manos,
a ver, a tener ojos,
a comer y llorar y derramarse
y amar y amar y sufrir y sufrir,
de aquella transición o escalofrío
del contenido eléctrico que asume
un cuerpo más como una copa viva,
y de aquella mujer deshabitada,
la madre que allí queda con su sangre
y su desgarradora plenitud
y su fin y comienzo, y el desorden
que turba el pulso, el suelo, las frazadas,
hasta que todo se recoge y suma
un nudo más el hilo de la vida,
nada, no quedó nada en tu memoria
del mar bravío que elevó una ola
y derribó del árbol una manzana oscura.

No tienes más recuerdo que tu vida.

a woman prepares to give birth.

It's well known that we were all born.

But of that abrupt translation
from not being to existing, to having hands,
to seeing, to having eyes,
to eating and weeping and overflowing
and loving and loving and suffering and suffering,
of that transition, that quivering
of an electric presence, raising up
one body more, like a living cup,
and of that woman left empty,
the mother who is left there in her blood
and her lacerated fullness,
and its end and its beginning, and disorder
tumbling the pulse, the floor, the covers
till everything comes together and adds
one knot more to the thread of life,
nothing, nothing remains in your memory
of the savage sea which summoned up a wave
and plucked a shrouded apple from the tree.

The only thing you remember is your life.

# Al difunto pobre

A nuestro pobre enterraremos hoy :
a nuestro pobre pobre.

Tan mal anduvo siempre
que es la primera vez
que habita este habitante.

Porque no tuvo casa, ni terreno,
ni alfabeto, ni sábanas,
ni asado,
y así de un sitio a otro, en los caminos,
se fue muriendo de no tener vida,
se fue muriendo poco a poco
porque esto le duró desde nacer.

Por suerte, y es extraño, se pusieron de acuerdo
todos desde el obispo hasta el juez
para decirle que tendrá cielo
y ahora muerto, bien muerto nuestro pobre,
ay nuestro pobre pobre
no va a saber qué hacer con tanto cielo.
Podrá ararlo y sembrarlo y cosecharlo ?

Él lo hizo simpre, duro
peleó con los terrones,
y ahora el cielo es suave para ararlo,
y luego entre los frutos celestiales
por fin tendrá lo suyo, y en la mesa
a tanta altura todo está dispuesto
para que coma cielo a dos carrillos
nuestro pobre que lleva, por fortuna,
sesenta años de hambre desde abajo

# To the Dead Poor Man

Today we are burying our own poor man;
our poor poor man.

He was always so badly off
that this is the first time
his person is personified.

For he had neither house nor land,
nor alphabet nor sheets,
nor roast meat,
and so from one place to another, on the roads,
he went, dying from lack of life,
dying little by little—
that was the way of it from his birth.

Luckily (and strangely) they were all of the same mind,
from the bishop to the judge,
in assuring him of his share of heaven;
and dead now, properly dead, our own poor man,
oh, our poor poor man,
he will not know what to do with so much sky.
Can he plow it or sow it or harvest it?

He did that always; cruelly
he struggled with raw land,
and now the sky lies easy to his plow,
and later, among the fruits of heaven,
he will have his share, and at his table,
at such a height, everything is set
for him to eat his fill of heaven,
our poor man, who brings, as his fortune
from below, some sixty years of hunger

para saciarla, al fin, como se debe,
sin recibir más palos de la vida,
sin que lo metan preso porque come,
bien seguro en su caja y bajo tierra
ya no se mueve para defenderse,
ya no combatirá por su salario.
Nunca esperó tanta justicia este hombre,
de pronto lo han colmado y lo agradece:
ya se quedó callado de alegría.

Qué peso tiene ahora el pobre pobre!
Era de puro hueso y de ojos negros
y ahora sabemos, por su puro peso,
ay cuántas cosas le faltaron siempre,
porque si este vigor anduvo andando,
cavando eriales, arañando piedras,
cortando trigo, remojando arcilla,
moliendo azufre, transportando leña,
si este hombre tan pesado no tenía
zapatos, oh dolor, si este hombre entero
de tendones y músculos no tuvo
nunca razón y todos le pegaron,
todos lo demolieron, y aún entonces
cumplió con sus trabajos, ahora llevándolo
en su ataúd sobre nosotros,
ahora sabemos cuánto le faltó
y no lo defendimos en la tierra.

Ahora nos damos cuenta que cargamos
con lo que no le dimos, y ya es tarde:

to be satisfied, finally, as is just and proper,
with no more batterings from life,
without being victimized for eating;
safe as houses in his box under the ground,
now he no longer moves to protect himself,
now he will not struggle over wages.
He never hoped for such justice, did this man.
Suddenly they have filled his cup and it cheers him;
now he has fallen dumb with happiness.

How heavy he is now, the poor poor man!
He was a bag of bones, with black eyes,
and now we know, by the weight of him alone,
the oh so many things he always lacked,
for if this strength had gone on and on,
digging up raw land, combing out stones,
harvesting wheat, soaking clay,
grinding down sulphur, lugging firewood,
if this so weighty man did not have shoes,
oh, misery, if this whole separate man
of tendon and muscle didn't ever have
justice in life, and all men beat him,
all men did him down, and even so
he went on laboring away, now, lifting him up,
in his coffin, on our shoulders,
now at least we know how much he didn't have,
that we did not help him in his life on earth.

Now it dawns on us we are taking on
all that we never gave him, and now it is late;

nos pesa y no podemos con su peso.

Cuántas personas pesa nuestro muerto?

Pesa como este mundo, y continuamos
llevando a cuestas este muerto. Es claro
que el cielo es una gran panadería.

he weighs on us, and we cannot take his weight.

How many people does our dead one weigh?

He weighs as much as this world does, and we go on
taking this dead one on our shoulders. It's clear
that heaven must abound in bread baking.

# A "La Sebastiana"

Yo construí la casa.

La hice primero de aire.
Luego subí en el aire la bandera
y la dejé colgada
del firmamento, de la estrella, de
la claridad y de la oscuridad.

Cemento, hierro, vidrio,
eran la fábula,
valían más que el trigo y como el oro,
había que buscar y que vender,
y así llegó un camión :
bajaron sacos
y más sacos,
la torre se agarró a la tierra dura
—pero, no basta, dijo el constructor,
falta cemento, vidrio, fierro, puertas—,
y no dormí en la noche.

Pero crecía,
crecían las ventanas
y con poco,
con pegarle al papel y trabajar
y arremeterle con rodilla y hombro
iba a crecer hasta llegar a ser,
hasta poder mirar por la ventana,
y parecía que con tanto saco
pudiera tener techo y subiría
y se agarrara, al fin, de la bandera

# To "La Sebastiana"

I built the house.

I made it first out of air.
Later I raised its flag into the air
and left it draped
from the firmament, from the stars, from
clear light and darkness.

It was a fable
of cement, iron, glass,
more valuable than wheat, like gold—
I had to go searching and selling,
and so a truck arrived.
They unloaded sacks
and more sacks.
The tower took anchor in the hard ground—
but that's not enough, said the Builder,
there's still cement, glass, iron, doors—
and I didn't sleep at night.

But it kept growing.
The windows grew,
and with a little more,
with sticking to plans and working,
and digging in with knee and shoulder,
it went on growing into existence,
to where you could look through a window,
and it seemed that with so many sacks
it might have a roof and might rise
and finally take firm hold of the flag

que aún colgaba del cielo sus colores.

Me dediqué a las puertas más baratas,
a las que habían muerto
y habían sido echadas de sus casas,
puertas sin muro, rotas,
amontonadas en demoliciones,
puertas ya sin memoria,
sin recuerdo de llave,
y yo dije: "Venid
a mí, puertas perdidas:
os daré casa y muro
y mano que golpea,
oscilaréis de nuevo abriendo el alma,
custodiaréis el sueño de Matilde
con vuestras alas que volaron tanto."

Entonces la pintura
llegó también lamiendo las paredes,
las vistió de celeste y de rosado
para que se pusieran a bailar.
Así la torre baila,
cantan las escaleras y las puertas,
sube la casa hasta tocar el mástil,
pero falta dinero:
faltan clavos,
faltan aldabas, cerraduras, mármol.
Sin embargo, la casa
sigue subiendo
y algo pasa, un latido
circula en sus arterias:
es tal vez un serrucho que navega

which still festooned the sky with its colors.

I gave myself over to the cheapest doors,
doors which had died
and had been pitched out of their houses,
doors without walls, broken,
piled up on scrap heaps,
doors with no memory by now,
no trace of a key,
and I said, "Come
to me, abandoned doors.
I'll give you a house and a wall
and a fist to knock on you.
You will swing again as the soul opens,
you will guard the sleep of Matilde
with your wings that worked so much."

Then, too, came the paint,
licking away at the walls;
it dressed them in sky blue and pink
so that they might begin to dance.
So the tower dances,
the doors and staircases sing,
the house rises till it touches its crown,
but money is short—
nails are short,
door knockers, locks, marble.
Nevertheless, the house
keeps on rising
and something happens, a beat
starts up in its arteries.
Perhaps it is a saw, seething

como un pez en el agua de los sueños
o un martillo que pica
como alevoso cóndor carpintero
las tablas del pinar que pisaremos.

Algo pasa y la vida continúa.

La casa crece y habla,
se sostiene en sus pies,
tiene ropa colgada en un andamio,
y como por el mar la primavera
nadando como náyade marina
besa la arena de Valparaíso,

ya no pensemos más : ésta es la casa :

ya todo lo que falta será azul,

lo que ya necesita es florecer.

Y eso es trabajo de la primavera.

like a fish in the water of dreams,
or a hammer which taps
like a tricky condor carpenter
at the pine planks we will be walking on.

Something goes and living continues.

The house grows and speaks,
stands on its own feet,
has clothes wrapped round its skeleton,
and as from seaward the spring,
swimming like a water nymph,
kisses the sand of Valparaíso,

now we can stop thinking. This is the house.

Now all that's missing will be blue.

All it needs now is to bloom.

And that is work for the spring.

# Adioses

Oh adioses a una tierra y otra tierra,
a cada boca y a cada tristeza,
a la luna insolente, a las semanas
que enrollaron los días y desaparecieron,
adiós a esta y aquella voz teñida
de amaranto, y adiós
a la cama y al plato de costumbre,
al sitio vesperal de los adioses,
a la silla casada con el mismo crepúsculo,
al camino que hicieron mis zapatos.

Me defundí, no hay duda,
me cambié de existencias,
cambié de piel, de lámpara, de odios,
tuve que hacerlo
no por ley ni capricho,
sino que por cadena,
me encadenó cada nuevo camino,
le tomé gusto a tierra a toda tierra.

Y pronto dije adiós, recién llegado,
con la ternura aún recién partida
como si el pan se abriera y de repente
huyera todo el mundo de la mesa.
Así me fui de todos los idiomas,
repetí los adioses como una puerta vieja,
cambié de cine, de razón, de tumba,
me fui de todas partes a otra parte,
seguí siendo y siguiendo
medio desmantelado en la alegría,
nupcial en la tristeza,

# Goodbyes

Goodbye, goodbye, to one place or another,
to every mouth, to every sorrow,
to the insolent moon, to weeks
which wound in the days and disappeared,
goodbye to this voice and that one stained
with amaranth, and goodbye
to the usual bed and plate,
to the twilit setting of all goodbyes,
to the chair that is part of the same twilight,
to the way made by my shoes.

I spread myself, no question;
I turned over whole lives,
changed skin, lamps, and hates,
it was something I had to do,
not by law or whim,
more of a chain reaction;
each new journey enchained me;
I took pleasure in place, in all places.

And, newly arrived, I promptly said goodbye
with still newborn tenderness
as if the bread were to open and suddenly
flee from the world of the table.
So I left behind all languages,
repeated goodbyes like an old door,
changed cinemas, reasons, and tombs,
left everywhere for somewhere else;
I went on being, and being always
half undone with joy,
a bridegroom among sadnesses,

ni saber nunca cómo ni cuándo
listo para volver, mas no se vuelve.

Se sabe que el que vuelve no se fue,
y así la vida anduve y desanduve
mudándome de traje y de planeta,
acostumbrándome a la compañía,
a la gran muchedumbre del destierro,
a la gran soledad de las campanas.

never knowing how or when,
ready to return, never returning.

It's well known that he who returns never left,
so I traced and retraced my life,
changing clothes and planets,
growing used to the company,
to the great whirl of exile,
to the great solitude of bells tolling.

## Para todos

De pronto no puedo decirte
lo que yo te debo decir,
hombre, perdóname, sabrás
que aunque no escuches mis palabras
no me eché a llorar ni a dormir
y que contigo estoy sin verte
desde hace tiempo y hasta el fin.

Yo comprendo que muchos piensen,
y qué hace Pablo? Estoy aquí.
Si me buscas en esta calle
me encontrarás con mi violín
preparado para cantar
y para morir.

No es cuestión de dejar a nadie
ni menos a aquéllos, ni a ti,
y si escuchas bien, en la lluvia,
podrás oír
que vuelvo y voy y me detengo.
Y sabes que debo partir.

Si no se saben mis palabras
no dudes que soy el que fui.
No hay silencio que no termine.
Cuando llegue el momento, espérame,
y que sepan todos que llego
a la calle, con mi violín.

# For Everyone

I can't just suddenly tell you
what I should be telling you,
friend, forgive me; you know
that although you don't hear my words,
I wasn't asleep or in tears,
that I'm with you without seeing you
for a good long time and until the end.

I know that many may wonder
''What is Pablo doing?'' I'm here.
If you look for me in this street
you'll find me with my violin,
prepared to break into song,
prepared to die.

It is nothing I have to leave to anyone,
not to these others, not to you,
and if you listen well, in the rain,
you'll hear
that I come and go and hang about.
And you know that I have to leave.

Even if my words don't know it,
be sure, I'm the one who left.
There is no silence which doesn't end.
When the moment comes, expect me
and let them all know I'm arriving
in the street, with my violin.

# La primavera

El pájaro ha venido
a dar la luz:
de cada trino suyo
nace el agua.

Y entre agua y luz que el aire desarrollan
ya está la primavera inaugurada,
ya sabe la semilla que ha crecido,
la raíz se retrata en la corola,
se abren por fin los párpados del polen.

Todo lo hizo un pájaro sencillo
desde una rama verde.

# Spring

The bird has come
to bring light to birth.
From every trill of his,
water is born.

And between water and light which unwind the air,
now the spring is inaugurated,
now the seed is aware of its own growing;
the root takes shape in the corolla,
at last the eyelids of the pollen open.

All this accomplished by a simple bird
from his perch on a green branch.

## A Don Asterio Alarcón
## cronometrista de Valparaíso

Olor a puerto loco
tiene Valparaíso
olor a sombra, a estrella,
a escama de la luna
y a cola de pescado.
El corazón recibe escalofríos
en las desgarradoras escaleras
de los hirsutos cerros:
allí grave miseria y negros ojos
bailan en la neblina
y cuelgan las banderas
del reino en las ventanas:
las sábanas zurcidas,
las viejas camisetas,
los largos calzoncillos,
y el sol del mar saluda los emblemas
mientras la ropa blanca balancea
un pobre adiós a la marinería.

Calles del mar, del viento,
del día duro envuelto en aire y ola,
callejones que cantan hacia arriba
en espiral como las caracolas:
la tarde comercial es transparente,
el sol visita las mercaderías,
para vender sonríe el almacén
abriendo escaparate y dentadura,
zapatos y termómetros, botellas
que encierran noche verde,
trajes inalcanzables, ropa de oro,
funestos calcetines, suaves quesos,
y entonces llego al tema

## To Don Asterio Alarcón,
## Clocksmith of Valparaíso


Smell of a crazy seaport,
Valparaíso has,
smell of shade, of stars,
a suspicion of the moon
and the tails of fish.
The heart takes to shivering
on the tattered stairways
up the shaggy hills.
There, squalor and black eyes
dance in the sea mist
and hang out the flags
of the kingdom in the windows—
the sheets stitched together,
the ancient undershirts,
the long-legged drawers—
and the sea sun salutes the emblems
while the white laundry waves
a threadbare goodbye to the sailors.

Streets of sea and wind,
of the hard day swaddled in air and waves,
alleyways singing upward
in a winding spiral, like shells—
the market afternoon is shining,
the sun touches the merchandise,
shop fronts smile like salesmen
opening windows and dentures,
shoes and thermometers, bottles
enclosing a green darkness,
impossible suits, clothes of gold,
gloomy socks, bland cheeses,
and now I get to the point

de esta oda.

Hay un escaparate
con su vidrio
y adentro,
entre cronómetros,
don Asterio Alarcón, cronometrista.
La calle hierve y sigue,
arde y golpea,
pero detrás del vidrio
el relojero,
el viejo ordenador de los relojes,
está inmovilizado
con un ojo hacia afuera,
un ojo extravagante
que adivina el enigma,
el cardíaco fin de los relojes
y escruta con un ojo
hasta que la impalpable mariposa
de la cronometría
se detiene en su frente
y se mueven las alas del reloj.

Don Asterio Alarcón es el antiguo
héroe de los minutos
y el barco va en la ola
medido por sus manos
que agregaron
responsabilidad al minutero,
pulcritud al latido:
Don Asterio en su acuario
vigiló los cronómetros del mar,
aceitó con paciencia

of this poem.

There is one window
with a glass eye
and inside,
among chronometers,
Don Asterio Alarcón, the clocksmith.
The street heaves and winds,
burns and bumps,
but behind the glass
the clocksmith,
the old curator of timepieces,
stands motionless
with a single protruding eye,
one amazing eye
which peers into the mystery,
the secret hearts of clocks,
and looks deeply in
until the elusive butterfly
of time in its measure
is trapped in his forehead
and the wings of the watch beat.

Don Asterio Alarcón is the ancient
hero of the minutes,
and boats go through the waves
governed by his fingers,
which gave to the minute hands
clockwork responsibilities,
and a meticulous tick.
Don Asterio in his aquarium
kept watch on the clocks of the sea,
oiled with patient fingers

el corazón azul de la marina.
Durante cincuenta años,
o dieciocho mil días,
allí pasaba el río
de niños y varones y mujeres
hacia harapientos cerros o hacia el mar,
mientras el relojero,
entre relojes,
detenido en el tiempo,
se suavizó como la nave pura
contra la eternidad de la corriente,
serenó su madera,
y poco a poco el sabio
salió del artesano,
trabajando
con lupa y con aceite
limpió la envidia, descartó el temor,
cumplió su ocupación y su destino,
hasta que ahora el tiempo,
el transcurrir temible,
hizo pacto con él, con don Asterio,
y él espera su hora de reloj.

Por eso cuando paso
la trepidante calle,
el río negro de Valparaíso,
sólo escucho un sonido entre sonidos,
entre tantos relojes uno solo :
el fatigado, suave, susurrante
y antiguo movimiento
de un gran corazón puro :
el insigne y humilde
tic tac de don Asterio.

the blue heart of the seaways.
For fifty steady years,
or eighteen thousand days,
a steady stream kept passing,
children and men and women,
up to the ragged hills or down to the sea,
while the clocksmith
among his clocks,
trapped in the flow of time,
kept smoothly on, as a ship does,
cleanly in the perpetual current,
pacified his wood,
and bit by bit the wise man
emerged from the artisan ;
working
with glass and oil,
he cleaned away hate, got rid of fear,
fulfilled his office and his destiny
to this present point where time,
that terrifying flow,
made its pact with him, with Don Asterio,
and he waits for his hour on the dial.

So, whenever I pass
along that vibrating street,
black river of Valparaíso,
I listen for one sound above the others,
one clock among so many clocks,
the tired, insistent, whispering,
and ancient movement
of a great and perfect heart,
the distinguished and humble
tick tock of Don Asterio.

# Oda a Acario Cotapos

De algún total sonoro
llegó al mundo Cotapos,
llegó con su planeta,
con su trueno,
y se puso a pasear por las ciudades
desenrollando el árbol de la música,
abriendo las bodegas del sonido.

Silencio! Caerá la ciudadela
porque de su insurrecta artillería
cuando menos se piensa y no se sabe
vuela el silencio súbito del cisne
y es tal el resplandor
que a su medida
toda el agua despierta,
todo rumor se ha convertido en ola,
todo salió a sonar con el rocío.

Pero, cuidad, cuidemos
el orden de esta oda
porque no sólo el aire se decide
a acompañar el peso de su canto
y no sólo las aves victoriosas
levantaron su vuelo en el estuario,
sino que entró y salió de las bodegas,
asimiló motores,
de la electricidad sacó la aurora
y la vistió de pompa y poderío.
Y aún más, de la tiniebla primordial
el músico regresa
con el lobo y el pasto pastoril,
con la sangre morada del centauro,

## To Acario Cotapos

Out of some rumbling wholeness,
Cotapos arrived in the world,
arrived with his whole planet,
with his thunder,
and began to stroll through cities
unwinding his tree of music,
opening storehouses of sound.

Silence! The citadel will fall
since from its rebellious batteries
when least expected, least realized,
flies the sudden silence of swans
and such is its radiance
that in its light
all the water awakes,
every rumor becomes a wave,
everything comes out to sing in the foam.

Careful, for we must watch
the order of this ode,
for it's not just air that decides
to share the touch of his song,
not just the triumphant birds
who took flight over the estuary—
it went in and out of storehouses,
it absorbed motors,
stole light from electricity
and dressed it in pomp and power.
Still more, out of primordial gloom
the music comes back,
bringing wolf and pastoral grass,
the purple blood of the centaur,

con el primer tambor de los combates
y la gravitación de las campanas.

Llega y sopla en su cuerno
y nos congrega,
nos cuenta,
nos inventa,
nos miente,
nos revela,
nos ata a un hilo sabio, a la sorpresa
de su certera lengua fabulosa,
nos equivoca y cuando
se va a apagar levanta
la mano y cae y sigue
la catarata insigne de su cuento.

Conocí de su boca
la historia natural de los enigmas,
el ave corolario,
el secreto teléfono
de los gatos, el viejo río
Mississippi con naves de madera,
el verdugo de Iván el Terrible,
la voz ancha de Boris Godunov,
las ceremonias de los ornitólogos
cuando lo condecoran en París,
el sagrado terror al hombre flaco,
el húmedo micrófono del perro,
la invocación nefasta
del señor Puga Borne,
el fox hunting en el condado
con chaquetilla roja y cup of tea,

the early drum of battle,
and the solemn weight of bells.

He arrives and blows on his horn,
and assembles us,
tells us,
invents us,
lies to us,
shows us,
winds us with wise thread, with the surprise
of his assured and fabulous language,
misleads us, and when
all is about to stop, he raises
his hand, and it falls, and there follows
the famous waterfall of his tale.

I came to know from his mouth
the natural history of all enigmas,
the corollary bird,
the secret telephone
of cats, the ancient river
Mississippi with its wooden boats,
Ivan the Terrible's hangman,
the huge voice of Boris Godunov,
the rituals of the ornithologists
when they honored him in Paris,
an unholy fear of skinny men,
the damp microphone of the dog,
the ominous invocation
of Señor Puga Borne,
fox-hunting in the county
with pink jacket and cup of tea,

el pavo que viajó a Leningrado
en brazos del benigno don Gregorio,
el desfile de los bolivianitos,
Ramón con su profundo calamar
y, sobre todo, la fatal historia
que Federico amaba
del Jabalí Cornúpeto
cuando
resoplando y roncando
creció y creció la bestia fabulosa
hasta que su irascible corpulencia
sobrepasó los límites de Europa
e inflada como inmenso Zeppelín
viajó al Brasil, en donde
agrimensores, ingenieros,
con peligro evidente de sus vidas,
la descendieron junto al Amazonas.

Cotapos, en tu música
se recompuso la naturaleza,
las aguas naturales,
la impaciencia del trueno,
y vi y toqué la luz en tus preludios
como si fueran hijos
de un cometa escarlata,
y en esa conmoción de tus campanas,
en esas fugas de tormenta y faro
los elementos hallan su medida
fraguando los metales de la música.

Pero hallé en tu palabra
la invicta alevosía

the turkey that traveled to Leningrad
in the arms of benign Don Gregorio,
the procession of little Bolivians,
Ramón with his solemn squid,
and most of all the awful story
which Federico loved
of Jabalí Cornúpeto
when,
puffing and roaring,
the fabulous beast grew and grew
until its testy corpulence
overflowed the borders of Europe
and, puffed up like a great Zeppelin,
it traveled to Brazil,
where surveyors and engineers,
at obvious risk to their lives,
brought it down beside the Amazon.

Cotapos, in your music
nature took new shape,
innocence of water,
irritation of thunder,
and I saw and touched light in your preludes
as if they were the children
of a scarlet comet,
and in the turbulence of your bells,
in those fugues of storms and lighthouses,
the elements find their measure,
forging the metal of music.

But I found in your vocabulary
the tireless trickery

del destructor de mitos y de platos,
la inesperada asociación que encuentra
en su camino el zorro hacia las uvas
cuando huele aire verde o pluma errante,
y no sólo
eso, sino
más :
la sinalefa eléctrica que muda
toda visión y cambian las palomas.

Tú, poeta sin libros,
juntaste en vida el canto irrespetuoso,
la palabra que salta de su cueva
donde yació sin sueño
y transformaste para mí el idioma
en un derrumbe de cristalerías.

Maestro, compañero,
me has enseñado tantas cosas claras
que donde estoy me das tu claridad.

Ahora,
escribo un libro de lo que yo soy
y en este soy, Acario, eres conmigo.

of a breaker of myths and plates,
the unexpected encounter which the fox has
on his way to the grapes
when he smells green air or a stray plum,
and not only
that but
more—
the electric metaphor
moved by whole visions, changed by doves.

You, poet without books,
brought together in life irreverent song,
and the word that sprang from the cave
where it lay dreamless,
and for me you turned language
into a landslide of glass houses.

Master, companion,
you have shown me so many clear things
that wherever I am, you give me your clarity.

Now,
I am writing a book about what I am,
and in this "I am," Acario, you are with me.

## Regresó el caminante

En plena calle me pregunto, dónde
está la ciudad? Se fue, no ha vuelto.
Tal vez ésta es la misma, y tiene casas,
tiene paredes, pero no la encuentro.
No se trata de Pedro ni de Juan,
ni de aquella mujer, ni de aquel árbol,
ya la ciudad aquella se enterró,
se metió en un recinto subterráneo
y otra hora vive, otra y no la misma,
ocupando la línea de las calles,
y un idéntico número en las casas.

El tiempo entonces, lo comprendo, existe,
existe, ya lo sé, pero no entiendo
cómo aquella ciudad que tuvo sangre,
que tuvo tanto cielo para todos,
y de cuya sonrisa a mediodía
se desprendía un cesto de ciruelas,
de aquellas casas con olor a bosque
recién cortado al alba con la sierra,
que seguía cantando junto al agua
de los aserraderos montañosos,
todo lo que era suyo y era mío,
de la ciudad y de la transparencia,
se envolvió en el amor como un secreto
y se dejó caer en el olvido.

Ahora donde estuvo hay otras vidas,
otra razón de ser y otra dureza :
todo está bien, pero por qué no existe ?
Por qué razón aquel aroma duerme ?
Por qué aquellas campanas se callaron

# The Wanderer Returned

In the middle of the street, I wonder, Where
is the city? It's gone, has not come back.
Perhaps this one is the same—it has houses,
it has walls, but I can't find it.
It isn't a matter of people—Pedro or Juan—
nor of that woman, nor of that tree;
now that city has buried itself,
has tumbled somewhere underground,
and this is another time, not the same at all,
taking on the same lines of streets,
assuming the same house numbers.

Time then does exist, I realize it.
I know it exists, but I cannot understand
how that city which had warm blood,
which had sky enough for all,
and whose midmorning smile
spread like a basketful of plums,
those houses with a forest smell,
wood newly cut at dawn with the saw,
the city that always sang at the water's edge
of sawmills in the mountains,
all that was yours and mine
of the city and its clarity,
wrapped itself up in love, secretly,
and let itself fall into forgetfulness.

Now where it once was there are other lives,
a different way of being, another hardness.
All is well enough, but why does it not exist?
Why is its old aroma now asleep?
Why did all those bells fall still,

y dijo adiós la torre de madera?

Tal vez en mí cayó casa por casa
la ciudad, con bodegas destruidas
por la lenta humedad, por el transcurso,
en mí cayó el azul de la farmacia,
el trigo acumulado, la herradura
que colgó de la talabartería,
y en mí cayeron seres que buscaban
como en un pozo el agua oscura.

Entonces yo a qué vengo, a qué he venido.
Aquella que yo amé entre las ciruelas
en el violento estío, aquella clara
como un hacha brillando con la luna,
la de ojos que mordían
como ácido el metal del desamparo,
ella se fue, se fue sin que se fuese,
sin cambiarse de casa ni frontera,
se fue en sí misma, se cayó en el tiempo
hacia atrás, y no cayó en los míos
cuando abría, tal vez, aquellos brazos
que apretaron mi cuerpo, y me llamaba
a lo largo, tal vez, de tantos años,
mientras yo en otra esquina del planeta
en mi distante edad me sumergía.

Acudiré a mí mismo para entrar,
para volver a la ciudad perdida.
En mí debo encontrar a los ausentes,
aquel olor de la maderería,
sigue creciendo sólo en mí tal vez

and why did the wooden tower say goodbye?

Perhaps the city fell away in me,
house by house, its warehouses eroded
by the slow damp, by passing time;
perhaps it was I who lost the blue of the pharmacy,
the stored-up wheat, the horseshoe
that hung in the harness store,
and those souls who were always searching
as though in a well of dark water.

Then what am I coming to, what have I come to?
That woman I loved once among the plums
in the stunning summer, clear, clear
as an ax blade catching the moon,
she with the eyes that bit
like acid into the metal of helplessness,
she went away, went away without leaving,
without changing house or country,
went of her own will, tumbling through time
backwards, and did not fall into mine
when she opened, possibly, those arms
which clasped my body, and she was calling me
perhaps at the distance of so many years,
while I, in another corner of the planet,
was drowning in the distance of my age.

I will ask leave of myself to enter,
to return to the missing city.
Inside myself I should find the absent ones,
that smell from the lumberyard;
perhaps the wheat that rippled on the slopes

el trigo que temblaba en la ladera
y en mí debo viajar buscando aquella
que se llevó la lluvia, y no hay remedio,
de otra manera nada vivirá,
debo cuidar yo mismo aquellas calles
y de alguna manera decidir
dónde plantar los árboles, de nuevo.

still goes on growing, but only within me,
and it's in myself I must travel to find that woman
the rain bore off, and there is no other way.
Nothing can last in any other way.
I am the one who must attend those streets
and somehow or other decide
where the trees should be planted, all over again.

# Alstromoeria

En este mes de enero la alstromoeria,
la sepultada flor, la sumergida,
de su secreto sube hacia los páramos.
Y amaneció rosado el roquerío.
Mis ojos reconocen
su marca triangular sobre la arena.
Yo me pregunto
viendo
el diente pálido
de un pétalo, el regazo
perfecto de sus íntimos lunares,
el suave fuego de su simetría,
cómo se preparó bajo la tierra?
Cómo donde no había sino polvo,
pedruscos o ceniza
surgió incitante, pura, aderezada,
encrespando en la vida su hermosura?
Cómo fue aquel trabajo subterráneo?
Cuándo se unió la forma con el polen?
Cómo a la oscuridad
llegó el rocío
y ascendió con la tierna llamarada
de la flor repentina
hasta que se tejieron gota a gota,
hilo por hilo las regiones secas
y por la luz rosada
pasó el aire esparciendo la fragancia
como si allí naciera
de pura tierra seca y abandono
fecundidad florida,

# Alstromeria

In this month of January, the alstromeria,
the flower entombed underground,
comes up out of hiding to the high wastes.
A blush of pink shows in the rock garden.
My eyes take in
its familiar triangle on the sand.
I wonder,
seeing
its pale petal
tooth, the perfect
cradle with its secret spots,
its smooth symmetrical fire—
how did it ready itself underground?
How, when there was nothing there but dust,
rocks, and ashes,
did it sprout, eager, clear, prepared,
protruding its grace into the world?
What was that underground labor like?
When did the form become one with the pollen?
How did the dew seep down
as far as that darkness
and the sudden flower ascend
like a warm flush of fire
till, drop by drop, thread by thread,
the dry places were mantled
and in the rosy light
the air moved, scattering fragrance,
as if from earth alone, dry and deserted,
there had sprung up
a fullness, a flowering,

frescura por amor multiplicada ?

Así pensé en enero
mirando el seco ayer mientras ahora
tímida y crespa crece
la tierna multitud de la alstromoeria :
y donde piedra y páramo
estuvieron
pasa el viento en su nave navegando
las olas olorosas.

a freshness multiplied by love?

So did I think in January,
looking at yesterday's dryness; while now,
timidly, crisply grows
the gentle multitude of alstromeria;
and across what once was stone
and dry plain,
the ship of the wind passes, rippling
the fragrant flowering waves.

# Indagaciones

Pregunté a cada cosa
si tenía
algo más,
algo más que la estructura
y así supe que nada era vacío:
todo era caja, tren, barco cargado
de multiplicaciones,
cada pie que pasó por un sendero
dejó escrito en la piedra un telegrama
y la ropa en el agua del lavado
dejó caer en gotas su existencia:
de clima en clima fui sin saber nunca
dónde dejar mi atado que pesaba
con los conocimientos que cargué,
hasta que tanto ver y conocer,
andar y andar, pregunta que pregunta
a cada silla, a cada piedra, y luego
a tantos hombres que no respondieron,
me acostumbraron a contestar solo:
a responderme sin haber hablado:
a conversar con nadie y divertirme.
Era tal vez lo que sucede al ciego
que de tanto no ver ya lo ve todo
y a un solo punto
mira
con la insistencia sólida del buzo
que baja a un solo pozo del océano
y allí todos los peces se congregan.

Pues bien, cuando dejé
de sacudir la tierra
y mover cada cosa de su sitio

# Investigations

I asked of every thing
if it had
something more,
something more than shape and form,
and I learned that way that nothing is empty—
everything is a box, a train, a boat
loaded with implications,
every foot that walked along a path
left a telegram written in the stone,
and clothes in the washing water
dripped out their whole existence.
I went from country to country, never knowing
where to put down my bundle, now so heavy,
loaded with all my knowings,
till with so much seeing and knowing,
moving and moving, asking and asking
every chair, every stone, and later
so many men who never answered,
they got me used to answering myself,
replying to myself without speaking,
talking with no one, to amuse myself.
Perhaps it's what happens to a blind man
who from so much not seeing then sees everything
and in a single focusing
sees
with all the intensity of a diver
who descends one single well in the whole ocean
and in that place all the fish are gathered.

Well then, when I left off
shaking the earth
and moving every thing from its place,

pensé que cada cual me halagaría
con un pequeño gracias o sonrisa
o parabién o paracualquier cosa,
mas no fue así y aquellos habitantes
de la ciudad terrible
alargaron un dedo,
un largo dedo muerto hacia mi vida
y con un ojo impune,
con un ojo de cíclope castrado
me vigilaron cuidadosamente:
"Disfruta de sus rentas clandestinas,"
dijo un astuto y criminal cadáver.
"Tiene automóvil," dijo una beata
con un escalofrío de dolor.
Y otro pasó vestido de poeta,
elegante y colérico conmigo
porque yo no cambiaba de camisa
y no tenía amor por su gerente.
Me dije, pues, las cosas de este modo
siguen siendo y tal vez
tienen razón:
pero de tan malvado
me resolví a seguir sin saber nada,
sin reclamar dos ojos por un ojo,
ni una mano por uña:
me decreté la dicha interminable
de que hablaran los pueblos por mi canto.

I thought that each of them would bestow on me
some little thank you or a smile,
or congratulations or whatever,
but it wasn't like that; and those inhabitants
of the terrible city
pointed a finger,
a long, dead finger, at my life
and with an indignant eye,
the eye of a castrated cyclops,
they scrutinized me thoughtfully.
"Make the best of your secret income,"
exclaimed one cunning and criminal corpse.
"He has a car," said one pious woman
with a shiver of pain.
And another passed, dressed as a poet,
most elegant, and furious with me
because I hadn't changed my shirt
and had no love for his manager.
At that point I said to myself
the things of this world just go on being
and perhaps they are right—
but from such corruption
I decided to go on knowing nothing,
not demanding two eyes for an eye
or a hand for a fingernail.
I made an unbreakable pledge to myself
that the people would find their voices in my song.

## C.O.S.C.

Ha muerto este mi amigo que se llamaba Carlos,
no importa quién, no pregunten, no saben,
tenía la bondad del buen pan en la mesa
y un aire melancólico de caballero herido.

No es él y es él, es todo, es la muerte que toca
la puerta,
de puro bueno salió a abrirle Carlos,
y entre tantos que abrieron esa noche la puerta
él solo quedó afuera,
él entre tantos hombres ahora ya no vuelve.
Y su ausencia me hiere como si me llamara,
como si continuara en la sombra esperándome.

Yo si hubiera escogido para este fin de un día
un dolor entre tantos que me acechan
no hubiera separado de la noche su rostro,
injustamente hubiera pasado sin recuerdo,
sin nombrarlo, y así no hubiera muerto
para mí, su cabeza continuaría gris
y sus tranquilos ojos que ahora ya no miran
seguirían abiertos en las torres de México.

De la muerte olvidar el más reciente ramo,
desconocer el rumbo, la proa o la bodega
en que mi amigo viaja solo o amontonado
y a esta hora creerlo aún dueño del día,
aún dueño de aquella claridad sonriente,
que repartió entre tantas tareas y personas.

Escribo estas palabras en mi libro pensando
que este desnudo adiós en que no está presente,

## C.O.S.C.

He has died, this friend of mine who was called Carlos.
Never mind who he was, don't ask if you don't know.
He had the goodness of good bread on the table
and the wistful air of a wounded gentleman.

It's not just him and it is him, it's everything,
it's death knocking at the door.
From sheer goodness, Carlos went to open it,
and out of so many who opened the door that night,
he was the one who stayed outside,
out of so many others he doesn't come back,
and his absence wounds me as if he were calling me,
as if he hung on in the shadow, expecting me.

If I had chosen for the end of this day
one grief among the many that hunt me out,
I would not have separated his face from the night ;
he would have cruelly passed out of memory,
without a name, and so would not have died for me,
his head would go on, gray,
and his gentle eyes, which now see nothing,
would still open on the towers of Mexico.

Just to forget this latest touching of death,
not to think of the course, the vessel, the hold
where my friend travels, alone or in a crowd,
and this moment to think of him, still lord of his day,
still lord of that smiling clarity
which he spread among so many troubles and people.

I write these words·down in my book, thinking
that this naked farewell, with him not present,

esta carta sencilla que no tiene respuesta,
no es nada sino polvo, nube, tinta, palabras
y la única verdad es que mi amigo ha muerto.

this simple letter, which cannot be answered,
is nothing more than dust, cloud, ink, and words
and the only truth is that my friend is dead.

## La noche en Isla Negra

Antigua noche y sal desordenada
golpean las paredes de mi casa:
sola es la sombra, el cielo
es ahora un latido del océano,
y cielo y sombra estallan
con fragor de combate desmedido:
toda la noche luchan
y nadie sabe el nombre
de la cruel claridad que se irá abriendo
como una torpe fruta:
así nace en la costa,
de la furiosa sombra, el alba dura,
mordida por la sal en movimiento,
barrida por el peso de la noche,
ensangrentada en su cráter marino.

# The Night in Isla Negra

Ancient night and the unruly salt
beat at the walls of my house.
The shadow is all one, the sky
throbs now along with the ocean,
and sky and shadow erupt
in the crash of their vast conflict.
All night long they struggle;
nobody knows the name
of the harsh light that keeps slowly opening
like a languid fruit.
So on the coast comes to light,
out of seething shadow, the harsh dawn,
gnawed at by the moving salt,
swept clean by the mass of night,
bloodstained in its sea-washed crater.

# Cardo

En
el
verano
del
largo
litoral,
por
polvorientas
leguas
y
caminos
sedientos
nacen las explosiones
del cardo azul de Chile.
Espolón
errabundo,
gran aguijón de moscardón morado,
pequeño pabellón de la hermosura,
todo el azul
levanta
una
copa
violeta
y,
árido,
hostil,
amargo,
el
seco
suelo
defiende
el fuego azul

# Thistle

In
the
summer
of the
long
shoreline,
along
dust-parched
miles
and
thirsty
back roads,
explodes into being
the blue thistle of Chile.
Wayward
groundspike,
great needle sting of the yellow hornet,
little castle of elegance,
all blueness
raises
a
violet
cup
and,
arid,
angry,
bitter,
the
stark
soil
defends
the blue fire

con
sus
espinas,
erizado
como un
alambre
y terco,
como
cerco
de ricos,
el
cardo
se
amontona
en
la
agresiva
fecundidad
del
matorral
salvaje
y empina
hacia
la indómita belleza
del territorio seco,
circundado
por vago cielo frío,
la sedición
azul
de sus corolas
como
invitando,

with
its
thorns,
bristling
like
wire
and harsh
like a
rich man's
fence,
the
thistle
crowds
round
in
the
savage
fertility
of the
wild
scrubland
and towers
toward
the ruthless beauty
of the dry wastes,
surrounded
by a blank, cold sky,
the blue
bravado
of its crowns
seeming to
call to,

como desafiando,
con un azul
más
duro
que
una
espada
a
todos
los azules
de
la
tierra.

seeming to challenge
with a blue
even
harder
than
a
sword blade
all
the
blues
of
the
earth.

# Pasado

Tenemos que echar abajo el pasado
y como se construye
piso por piso, ventana a ventana,
y sube el edificio
así, bajando vamos
primero tejas rotas,
luego orgullosas puertas,
hasta que del pasado
sale polvo
como si se golpeara
contra el suelo,
sale humo
como si se quemara,
y cada nuevo día
reluce
como un plato
vacío:
no hay nada, no hubo nada:
hay que llenarlo
de nuevas nutriciones
espaciosas,
entonces, hacia abajo
cae el día de ayer
como en un pozo
al agua del pasado,
a la cisterna
de lo que ya no tiene voz ni fuego.
Es difícil
acostumbrar los huesos
a perderse,
los ojos
a cerrarse
pero

# Past

We have to discard the past
and, as one builds
floor by floor, window by window,
and the building rises,
so do we keep shedding—
first, broken tiles,
then proud doors,
until, from the past,
dust falls
as if it would crash
against the floor,
smoke rises
as if it were on fire,
and each new day
gleams
like an empty
plate.
There is nothing, there was always nothing.
It all has to be filled
with a new, expanding
fruitfulness;
then, down
falls yesterday
as in a well
falls yesterday's water,
into the cistern
of all that is now without voice, without fire.
It is difficult
to get bones used
to disappearing,
to teach eyes
to close,
but

lo hacemos
sin saberlo:
todo era vivo,
vivo, vivo, vivo
como un pez escarlata
pero el tiempo
pasó con trapo y noche
y fue borrando
el pez y su latido:
al agua al agua al agua
va cayendo el pasado
aunque se agarre
a espinas
y raíces:
se fue se fue y no valen
los recuerdos:
ya el párpado sombrío
cubrió la luz del ojo
y aquello que vivía
ya no vive:
lo que fuimos no somos.
Y la palabra aunque las letras tengan
iguales transparencias y vocales
ahora es otra y es otra la boca:
la misma boca es otra boca ahora:
cambiaron labios, piel, circulaciones,
otro ser ocupó nuestro esqueleto:
aquel que fue en nosotros ya no está:
se fue, pero si llaman, respondemos
''Aquí estoy'' y se sabe que no estamos,
que aquel que estaba, estuvo y se perdió:
se perdió en el pasado y ya no vuelve.

we do it
unwittingly.
Everything was alive,
alive, alive, alive
like a scarlet fish,
but time
passed with cloth and darkness
and kept wiping away
the flash of the fish.
Water water water,
the past goes on falling
although it keeps a grip
on thorns
and on roots.
It went, it went, and now
memories mean nothing.
Now the heavy eyelid
shut out the light of the eye
and what was once alive
is now no longer living;
what we were, we are not.
And with words, although the letters
still have transparency and sound,
they change, and the mouth changes;
the same mouth is now another mouth;
they change, lips, skin, circulation;
another soul took on our skeleton;
what once was in us now is not.
It left, but if they call, we reply
"I am here," and we realize we are not,
that what was once, was and is lost,
lost in the past, and now does not come back.

# A E.S.S.

Cinco años
de E.,
luego seis años,
ahora nueve y medio
siempre aquí entre las algas
de Isla Negra,
entre ola y ola un niño
con la curiosidad del universo
que se abre aquí como corola verde
con todo el mar
golpeando los ojos peregrinos
y, hierba de agua y cerro,
un año más de Enrique,
de Segura,
de Salazar, el nieto de don Cloro.
Sabrás más tarde
que vi
cómo crecías
como si me mirara
una pestaña,
algo íntimo,
interno como el pulso,
y cada vez de tan largos transcursos
al ir a poner pie sobre mi arena
creciendo
apareciste
y subían tus meses,
tus años, uno a uno, de la tierra
y entrabas en la casa
con más tiempo en los ojos
y más piernas,
un centímetro más que levantaba

## To E.S.S.

Enrique,
five years old,
then six,
now nine and a half,
always here among the seaweed
of Isla Negra,
between waves a child
with a whole world of curiosity
opening here like a green corolla
with the whole sea
beating on his wandering eyes
and, grass of water and hillside,
another year of Enrique,
Enrique de Segura
Salazar, Don Cloro's grandson.
Later you will be aware
that I saw
how you were growing
as if I were in touch with
an eyelash,
something intimate,
something internal, like a pulse,
and each time, at such a stretch of time
as you left your footprints across my sand,
growing,
you appeared
and they mounted up, your months,
your years, one by one on the earth,
and you came into the house
with more time in your eyes
and more leg length,
an extra centimeter which lifted

tu corazón de pájaro con trinos
un poco más arriba hacia el follaje,
hacia el árbol oscuro de la vida.
Y ahora con nueve años
de Enrique
aquí en el abandono de la costa
oh pequeño astronauta
te pregunto, y pregunto:
volarás en tu nave
alguna vez,
veloz como ninguno entre los ojos
de Orión que parpadean
invitándote?
Irá tu carro ardiendo
por las calles de las constelaciones,
nos traerás las algas de la luna,
de Aldebarán la piedra misteriosa,
y de la Osa Mayor una guitarra?
Ay niño
de esta arena,
Enrique de estos páramos marinos,
tal vez, no irás adonde,
ni volverás jamás del sinembargo
y entre dunas y adobes
transcurrirá la línea
de una vida, terrón de arcilla espesa
sin castillo ni luna,
línea quebrada como
el litoral
herido
que desangra entre las piedras perdidas
las llaves de la cólera, la espuma

your chirping bird heart
a little higher toward the foliage,
toward the shadowy tree of all life.
And now with nine years
of Enrique
here in the wasteland of the coast,
oh, little astronaut,
I ask you and I ask—
will you fly in your spaceship
sometime,
swifter than anything, between the eyes
of Orion which wink
invitingly at you?
Will your fiery coach flash
through the streets of the constellations;
will you bring us seaweed from the moon,
mysterious stones from Aldebaran,
a guitar from the Great Bear?
Oh, child
of this shore,
Enrique of these seaside wastes,
perhaps you will not go to these wherevers,
nor ever come back from your wherefores,
and between dune and adobe,
the line of one life will happen,
a lump of solid clay
with neither castle nor moon,
a broken line like
the despoiled
seashore
which bleeds off among abandoned stones
the keys of its rage, the spume

del vaivén tumultuoso
que viene y va y se queda
convertido en la arena
del olvido.

of its thunderous coming and going
which comes and goes and stays
changed into the sand
of forgetting.

## Al mismo puerto

Valparaíso tiene hilos,
copas de largo alcance,
redes entrelazadas.
Y bajo la espesura
de todo el mar cuando se desarrolla
y crecen una a una las escamas
de solitarios peces,
o donde los arpones
ensangrentados duermen palpitando
sueños de sal y sangre.
O más allá, en el pecho
del poeta,
Valparaíso cava
y busca y halla
y abre y deja
una red emboscada
en la firmeza:
entonces vuelan imprevistas lanzas,
máquinas
amarillas,
los hambrientos fuegos petreles,
la habitación sin rumbo
entre los cerros,
sostenida
por un pétalo puro de pintura.
Y también en el cielo
el ave atardecida,
o el ciclónico avión endurecido
como bala de luna,
todo
arriba
recibe
la emanación portuaria,

# To the Same Port

Valparaíso has feelers,
cups with a huge capacity,
interlacing nets.
And underneath the tangle
of the whole sea when it unrolls,
where the scales of single fish
are growing, one by one,
or where bloodstained harpoons
rest asleep, quivering
with dreams of blood and salt,
or further away, into the heart
of the poet,
Valparaíso penetrates
and searches and finds
and opens and leaves
a net hidden
in the continuity;
then surprising lances go flying,
yellow
machines,
the hungry petrels,
the meager room
among the hills,
sustained by
one clear painted petal.
And in the sky too,
the bird of afternoon
or the hurtling plane, tempered
like a bullet from the moon,
all things
above
feel
the fine waves from the port,

y sigilosa
la estrella se dirige
a la pobre bahía,
a las casas colgadas,
al duelo, al desamparo,
a la alegría
del fin del mar, de la sirena pobre,
de la ciudad marina
que el océano atroz no desmorona
ni sepultó el castigo de la tierra.

Tiene Valparaíso
correspondencias negras con el viento,
deudas con el rocío,
agujeros que no tienen respuestas,
explícitos alcaldes que pasean
perritos tristes al atardecer,
domingos silenciosos de sarcófago:
pero no importa, todo
se comprende
cuando por tierra o mar o cielo o hilo
se siente un golpe como
cucharada:
algo llama, algo cae,
polvo frágil de sueño,
latido o luz del agua,
imperceptible
signo,
harina
o sal nocturna.
Y allí mismo doblamos
la mirada
hacia Valparaíso.

and silently
the star turns itself
toward the sparse bay,
to the suspended houses,
to grief, to helplessness,
to all the joy
of the sea's edge, of the poor siren,
of the marine city
which the brutal sea has not worn down,
which the punishing land has not buried.

Valparaíso has
black connections with the wind,
debts with the dew,
holes which cannot be answered,
precise mayors who walk
their sad dogs in the afternoons,
silent, tomb-like Sundays—
but no matter, everything,
everything comes clear
when across earth or sea or sky or wire
you feel a shock, a sudden
interruption—
something calls, something falls,
faint dust from a dream,
a beat, light from the water,
an imperceptible
signal,
flour
or salt of the night.
And at that point we turn
our gaze toward
Valparaíso.

# A la tristeza / II

Tristeza, necesito
tu ala negra,
tanto sol, tanta miel en el topacio,
cada rayo sonríe
en la pradera
y todo es luz redonda en torno mío,
todo es abeja eléctrica en la altura.
Por eso
tu ala negra
dame,
hermana tristeza :
necesito que alguna vez se apague
el zafiro y que caiga
la oblicua enredadera de la lluvia,
el llanto de la tierra :
quiero
aquel madero roto en el estuario.
la vasta casa a oscuras
y mi madre
buscando
parafina
y llenando la lámpara
hasta no dar la luz sino un suspiro.

La noche no nacía.

El día resbalaba
hacia su cementerio provinciano,
y entre el pan y la sombra
me recuerdo
a mí mismo
en la ventana

# To Sadness / II

Sadness, I need
your black wing.
So much sun, so much honey in the topaz,
each ray smiling
in the wide fields
and all an abundant light about me,
all a whirring bee in the high air.
And so
give me
your black wing,
sister sadness,
I need sometimes to have the sapphire
extinguished and to have
the angled mesh of the rain fall,
the weeping of the earth;
I long for
that battered hulk in the estuary,
the great house in darkness,
and my mother
searching
for paraffin
and filling the lamp
till it gave out, not light, but a sigh.

The night was not born.

The day was withdrawing
to its own local cemetery,
and between the bread and the shadow
I have a memory
of myself
in the window

mirando lo que no era,
lo que no sucedía
y un ala negra de agua que llegaba
sobre aquel corazón que allí tal vez
olvidé para siempre, en la ventana.

Ahora echo de menos
la luz negra.

Dame tu lenta sangre,
lluvia
fría,
dame tu vuelo atónito!
A mi pecho
devuélvele la llave
de la puerta cerrada,
destruida.
Por un minuto, por
una corta vida,
quítame luz y déjame
sentirme
perdido y miserable,
temblando entre los hilos
del crepúsculo,
recibiendo en el alma
las manos
temblorosas
de
la
lluvia.

looking at what was not,
at what was not happening,
and a black wing of water coming down
across that heart which there perhaps
I forgot forever, there in the window.

Now I am missing
the black light.

Give me your slow blood,
cold
rain,
spread over me your fearful wing!
Into my care
give back the key
of the closed door,
the ruined door.
For a moment, for
a short lifetime,
remove my light and leave me
to feel myself
abandoned, wretched,
trembling in the web
of twilight,
receiving into my being
the quivering
hands
of
the
rain.

# Sumario

Estoy contento con tantos deberes
que me impuse, en mi vida
se amasaron extraños materiales :
tiernos fantasmas que me despeinaban,
categóricas manos minerales,
un viento sin razón que me agitaba,
la espina de unos besos lacerantes, la dura realidad
de mis hermanos,
mi deber imperioso de vigía,
mi inclinación a ser sólo yo mismo
en la debilidad de mis placeres,
por eso —agua en la piedra— fue mi vida
cantando entre la dicha y la dureza.

# Summary

I am pleased at having taken on
so many obligations—in my life
most curious elements accumulated:
gentle ghosts which undid me,
an insistent mineral labor,
an inexplicable wind which ruffled me,
the stab of some wounding kisses, the hard reality
of my brothers,
my insistent need to be always watchful,
my impulse to be myself, only myself
in the weakness of self-pleasuring.
That is why—water on stone—my life was always
singing its way between joy and obligation.

# El pueblo

De aquel hombre me acuerdo y no han pasado
sino dos siglos desde que lo vi,
no anduvo ni a caballo ni en carroza:
a puro pie
deshizo
las distancias
y no llevaba espada ni armadura,
sino redes al hombro,
hacha o martillo o pala,
nunca apaleó a ninguno de su especie:
su hazaña fue contra el agua o la tierra,
contra el trigo para que hubiera pan,
contra el árbol gigante para que diera leña,
contra los muros para abrir las puertas,
contra la arena construyendo muros
y contra el mar para hacerlo parir.

Lo conocí y aún no se me borra.

Cayeron en pedazos las carrozas,
la guerra destruyó puertas y muros,
la ciudad fue un puñado de cenizas,
se hicieron polvo todos los vestidos,
y él para mí subsiste,
sobrevive en la arena,
cuando antes parecía
todo imborrable menos él.

En el ir y venir de las familias
a veces fue mi padre o mi pariente
o apenas si era él o si no era
tal vez aquel que no volvió a su casa

# The People

That man I remember well, and at least two centuries
have passed since I last saw him;
he traveled neither on horseback nor in a carriage,
always on foot
he undid
the distances,
carrying neither sword nor weapon
but nets on his shoulder,
ax or hammer or spade;
he never fought with another of his kind—
his struggle was with water or with earth,
with the wheat, for it to become bread,
with the towering tree, for it to yield wood,
with walls, to open doors in them,
with sand, to form it into walls,
and with the sea, to make it bear fruit.

I knew him and he goes on haunting me.

The carriages splintered into pieces,
war destroyed doorways and walls,
the city was a fistful of ashes,
all the dresses shivered into dust,
and for me he persists,
he survives in the sand,
when everything previously
seemed durable except him.

In the comings and goings of families,
sometimes he was my father or my relative
or almost was, or, if not, perhaps
the other one who never came back home

porque el agua o la tierra lo tragaron
o lo mató una máquina o un árbol
o fue aquel enlutado carpintero
que iba detrás del ataúd, sin lágrimas,
alguien en fin que no tenía nombre,
que se llamaba metal o madera,
y a quien miraron otros desde arriba
sin ver la hormiga
sino el hormiguero
y que cuando sus pies no se movían,
porque el pobre cansado había muerto,
no vieron nunca que no lo veían:
había ya otros pies en donde estuvo.

Los otros pies eran él mismo,
también las otras manos,
el hombre sucedía:
cuando ya parecía transcurrido
era el mismo de nuevo,
allí estaba otra vez cavando tierra,
cortando tela, pero sin camisa,
allí estaba y no estaba, como entonces,
se había ido y estaba de nuevo,
y como nunca tuvo cementerio,
ni tumba, ni su nombre fue grabado
sobre la piedra que cortó sudando,
nunca sabía nadie que llegaba
y nadie supo cuando se moría,
así es que sólo cuando el pobre pudo
resucitó otra vez sin ser notado.

Era el hombre sin duda, sin herencia,

because water or earth swallowed him,
a machine or a tree killed him,
or he was that funeral carpenter
who walked behind the coffin, dry-eyed,
someone who never had a name
except as wood or metal have names,
and on whom others looked from above,
not noticing the ant,
only the anthill;
so that when his feet no longer moved
because, poor and tired, he had died,
they never saw what they were not used to seeing—
already other feet walked in his footsteps.

The other feet were still him,
the other hands as well.
The man persisted.
When it seemed he must be spent,
he was the same man over again;
there he was once more, digging the ground,
cutting cloth, but without a shirt,
he was there and he wasn't, just as before
he had gone away and replaced himself;
and since he never had cemetery
or tomb, or his name engraved
on the stone that he sweated to cut,
nobody ever knew of his arrival
and nobody knew when he died,
so only when the poor man was able
did he come back to life, unnoticed.

He was the man all right, with no inheritance,

sin vaca, sin bandera,
y no se distinguía entre los otros,
los otros que eran él,
desde arriba era gris como el subsuelo,
como el cuero era pardo,
era amarillo cosechando trigo,
era negro debajo de la mina,
era color de piedra en el castillo,
en el barco pesquero era color de atún
y color de caballo en la pradera:
cómo podía nadie distinguirlo
si era el inseparable, el elemento,
tierra, carbón o mar vestido de hombre?

Donde vivió crecía
cuanto el hombre tocaba:
la piedra hostil,
quebrada
por sus manos,
se convertía en orden
y una a una formaron
la recta claridad del edificio,
hizo el pan con sus manos,
movilizó los trenes,
se poblaron de pueblos las distancias,
otros hombres crecieron,
llegaron las abejas,
y porque el hombre crea y multiplica
la primavera caminó al mercado
entre panaderías y palomas.

El padre de los panes fue olvidado,

no cattle, no coat of arms,
and he did not stand out from others,
others who were himself;
from above he was gray, like clay,
he was drab, like leather,
he was yellow harvesting wheat,
he was black down in the mine,
stone-colored in the castle,
in the fishing boat the color of tuna,
horse-colored on the prairies—
how could anyone distinguish him
if he were inseparable from his element,
earth, coal, or sea in a man's form?

Where he lived, everything
the man touched would grow—
the hostile stones
broken
by his hands
took shape and line
and one by one assumed
the sharp forms of buildings;
he made bread with his hands,
set the trains running;
the distances filled with towns,
other men grew,
the bees arrived,
and through the man's creating and multiplying,
spring wandered into the marketplace
between bakeries and doves.

The father of the loaves was forgotten,

él que cortó y anduvo, machacando
y abriendo surcos, acarreando arena,
cuando todo existió ya no existía,
él daba su existencia, eso era todo.
Salió a otra parte a trabajar, y luego
se fue a morir rodando
como piedra del río:
aguas abajo lo llevó la muerte.

Yo, que lo conocí, lo vi bajando
hasta no ser sino lo que dejaba:
calles que apenas pudo conocer,
casas que nunca y nunca habitaría.

Y vuelvo a verlo, y cada día espero.

Lo veo en su ataúd y resurrecto.

Lo distingo entre todos
los que son sus iguales
y me parece que no puede ser,
que así no vamos a ninguna parte,
que suceder así no tiene gloria.

Yo creo que en el trono debe estar
este hombre, bien calzado y coronado.

Creo que los que hicieron tantas cosas
deben ser dueños de todas las cosas.
Y los que hacen el pan deben comer!

Y deben tener luz los de la mina!

the one who cut and trudged, beating
and opening paths, shifting sand ;
when everything came into being, he no longer existed.
He gave away his existence, that was all.
He went somewhere else to work and ultimately
he went toward death, rolling
like a river stone ;
death carried him off downstream.

I who knew him saw him go down
until he existed only in what he was leaving—
streets he could scarcely be aware of,
houses he never never would inhabit.

And I come back to see him, and every day I wait.

I see him in his coffin and resurrected.

I pick him out from all
the others who are his equals
and it seems to me that this cannot be,
that this way leads us nowhere,
that to continue so has no glory.

I believe that heaven must encompass
this man, properly shod and crowned.

I think that those who made so many things
ought to be owners of everything.
That those who make bread ought to eat.

That those in the mine should have light.

Basta ya de encadenados grises!

Basta de pálidos desaparecidos!

Ni un hombre más que pase sin que reine.

Ni una sola mujer sin su diadema.

Para todas las manos guantes de oro.

Frutas de sol a todos los oscuros!

Yo conocí aquel hombre y cuando pude,
cuando ya tuve ojos en la cara,
cuando ya tuve la voz en la boca
lo busqué entre las tumbas, y le dije
apretándole un brazo que aún no era polvo:

"Todos se irán, tú quedarás viviente.

Tú encendiste la vida.

Tú hiciste lo que es tuyo."

Por eso nadie se moleste cuando
parece que estoy solo y no estoy solo,
no estoy con nadie y hablo para todos:

Alguien me está escuchando y no lo saben,
pero aquellos que canto y que lo saben
siguen naciendo y llenarán el mundo.

Enough now of gray men in chains!

Enough of the pale lost ones!

Not another man should pass except as a ruler.

Not one woman without her diadem.

Gloves of gold for every hand.

Fruits of the sun for all the shadowy ones!

I knew that man, and when I could,
when I still had eyes in my head,
when I still had a voice in my throat,
I sought him among the tombs and I said to him,
pressing his arm that still was not dust:

''Everything will pass, you will still be living.

You set fire to life.

You made what is yours.''

So let no one be perturbed when
I seem to be alone and am not alone;
I am not without company and I speak for all.

Someone is hearing me without knowing it,
but those I sing of, those who know,
go on being born and will overflow the world.

# Plenos poderes

A puro sol escribo, a plena calle,
a pleno mar, en donde puedo canto,
sólo la noche errante me detiene
pero en su interrupción recojo espacio,
recojo sombra para mucho tiempo.

El trigo negro de la noche crece
mientras mis ojos miden la pradera
y así de sol a sol hago las llaves:
busco en la oscuridad las cerraduras
y voy abriendo al mar las puertas rotas
hasta llenar armarios con espuma.

Y no me canso de ir y de volver,
no me para la muerte con su piedra,
no me canso de ser y de no ser.

A veces me pregunto si de donde
si de padre o de madre o cordillera
heredé los deberes minerales,

los hilos de un océano encendido
y sé que sigo y sigo porque sigo
y canto porque canto y porque canto.

No tiene explicación lo que acontece
cuando cierro los ojos y circulo
como entre dos canales submarinos,
uno a morir me lleva en su ramaje
y el otro canta para que yo cante.

Así pues de no ser estoy compuesto

## Fully Empowered

I write in the clear sun, in the teeming street,
at full sea tide, in a place where I can sing;
only the wayward night inhibits me,
but, interrupted by it, I recover space,
I gather shadows to last a long time.

The black crop of the night is growing
while my eyes in the meantime measure the plain.
So, from sun to sun, I forge the keys.
In the half light I look for locks
and keep on opening broken doors to the sea
until I fill the cupboards up with foam.

And I never weary of going and returning.
Death in its stone aspect does not stop me.
I am weary neither of being nor of non-being.

Sometimes I wonder where—
from father or mother or the mountains—
I inherited all my mineral obligations,

the threads spreading from a sea on fire;
and I know I go on and go on because I go on
and I sing because I sing and because I sing.

There is no way of explaining what happens
when I close my eyes and waver
as between two underwater channels—
one lifts me in its branches toward dying
and the other sings in order that I may sing.

And so I am formed out of non-being,

y como el mar asalta el arrecife
con cápsulas saladas de blancura
y retrata la piedra con la ola,
así lo que en la muerte me rodea
abre en mí la ventana de la vida
y en pleno paroxismo estoy durmiendo.
A plena luz camino por la sombra.

and as the sea goes battering at a reef
in wave on wave of salty white-tops
and drags back stones in its ebb,
so what there is of death surrounding me
opens in me a window out to living,
and, in a spasm of being, I am asleep.
In the full light of day, I walk in the shade.